HOGAN'S HOPE
Finding a Forever Home of Love and Acceptance

Connie Bombaci
Illustrated by Heather Ferrer

Based on a True Story

Husky Trail Press LLC

ISBN 978-1-935258-60-5

Edited by Gayle Byrne

Husky Trail Press LLC
PO Box 421214
Kissimmee, FL 34742-1214
info@huskytrailpress.com
www.HuskyTrailPress.com

To my loving family
and all the precious creatures
who have brought greater joy
and
deeper understanding into my life.

With hope, amazing things are possible!

Be on the lookout, in the illustrations,
for Ten's four special dots on the top of his head.

The hope for springtime arrived, and the breeze whispered, "Warmer days are coming!"

Suddenly, the wind gusted, and the backdoor shouted, "Bang! Bang! Bang!" and the dog cages hollered, "Clang! Clang! Clang!" as they swung open and shut.

No one was home at the Brown family's farmhouse.

Vicki sat in the yard and expected her puppies to be born at any moment.

Lifting her nose to sniff the air, she felt cold in the icy wind.

Gigantic snowflakes fell, and one even landed on her nose.

Vicki forced her way through a hole in the barn wall to get out of the storm and protect her puppies.

One...Two...Three...One-by-one, the puppies were born and licked clean by their mama who pulled them close for safety and warmth.

Soon, the Brown family returned home, and their little girl, Anna, leaped out of the car and dashed to see Vicki. Anna squealed when she saw the last – the tenth - puppy being born.

He was the smallest one who tilted his head to look straight into Anna's eyes. He seemed different, but Anna knew that being different made him extra special. She named him Number Ten thinking, "Vicki saved the best for last."

 Thoughts: How do you think Number is different? What makes you different and special?

Every day, the white puppies grew bigger. They started playing, pouncing on each other's backs, and chasing their tails.

Being Dalmatians, their black spots began to magically appear.

Number Ten hoped to be just like the other puppies
and get his spots, too.

 Thought: Did you know that Dalmatian puppies
are born without their spots?

When the puppies were eight-weeks-old, Anna's father put up a sign telling families that they could come and buy a puppy to take home.

Number Ten hoped to get a forever home, too.

But first, the puppies had to go for their checkups at the veterinarian's.

Anna crawled into the crates, telling the puppies, "Follow me!"

As Dr. O watched and examined Number Ten, he scratched his head and asked, "Does Ten come when you call him? I think he might be deaf."

Anna guessed that Ten was different and believed with all her heart that being different meant being special!

Ten did not know that he was different and only **hoped** to be loved.

Nobody wanted a deaf dog. So Anna bravely asked her father, "May I keep Number Ten? Please?!"

Mr. Brown stayed quiet, and Anna breathlessly waited. Suddenly, he shouted, "Okay, but...

One: No dogs in the house!
Two: You must do everything to take care of him!"

Ten hoped to stay with Anna who he loved with all his heart.

Summer flew by. June became July, and July became August. Anna had to go back to school.

Before she hurried to get on the bus, she kissed Ten's forehead and promised, "I will be back."

Ten wondered where Anna was going and watched the school bus disappear in the dust.

Ten hoped that Anna would come back.

The days seemed so long as he watched and waited.

Ten hoped to have someone spend time with him.

Ten felt sad and lonely outside by himself,
and Anna worried about her puppy.

Because she loved him so much, Anna hoped to find Ten a
forever home where he could be inside with everyone.

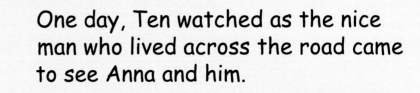

One day, Ten watched as the nice man who lived across the road came to see Anna and him.

Anna and the man hoped to find Ten a forever home where he could live inside with lots of love and attention.

16

What a surprise when the man lifted Ten up into his truck for a ride!

Leaning over the seat, Ten hoped that he was going to a place filled with love and a family to keep him company.

 Thought: What do you hope happens to Number Ten?

Ten got more surprises! He went inside the man's home and even discovered a cozy bed made just for him.

Ten hoped that he would always be allowed inside with a soft place to sleep.

Ten believed that anything is possible if he hoped. And... his dream to cuddle with someone all night long came true!

 Thought: What dream do you have that you want to come true?

The next morning, Ten found a ginormous bowl of yummy breakfast and gobbled down every crumb.

Ten hoped that his tummy would always feel full.

Next, the nice man took Ten to see the friendly woman at the rescue shelter where families went to adopt pets.

As she gently patted his head, she exclaimed, "I know the perfect family to call for you!"

Ten hoped for a forever home that wanted him just the way he was.

Ten's hope came true!

He went home with a new mama, papa, and four-legged sister named India.

India hoped and always dreamed for her very own brother!

Ten and India loved playing and laying in the grass together.

 Thought: Do you think India cared that Ten was deaf?

Because Ten could not hear their voices, Mama and Papa decided to talk to him with their hands by teaching him sign language.

Cookie
Turn cupped hand like a cookie cutter

Sit
Place fingers like legs over a chair

Ten hoped to be like everyone and understand what people said to him.

 Thought: Can you say these words with your hands?

Mama and Papa changed Ten's name to Hogan, which means shelter because they promised that he would always be allowed to go inside a warm, loving home.

Hogan loved that anyone, including children, could sign to him.

Mama

Papa

Hogan believed that anything is possible when we hope.

Hogan loved being happy and learning new signs.

One of his favorites was the word "kiss," and he gave puppy kisses to everyone.

Kiss

Touch lips then cheek

 Thought: Do you like puppy kisses?

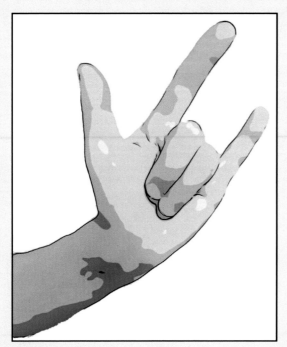

I Love You

Stay

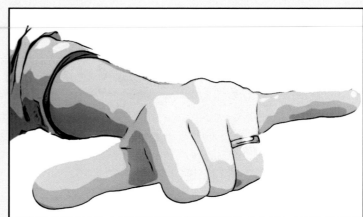

Hogan never gave up hope for love and acceptance!

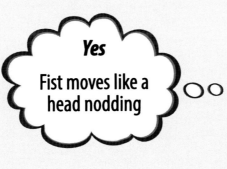

Yes

Fist moves like a head nodding

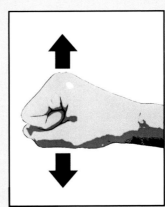

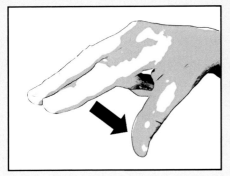

No

Tap two fingers to thumb

Walk

Fingers move like legs walking

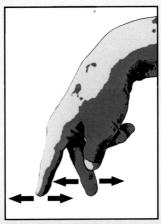

 Thoughts: What is your favorite sign?
How many words do you think Hogan learned?

Hogan's dream for a loving forever home came true.

With hope, anything is possible!

Hogan hoped that we all love and accept each other, no matter what, and believe that dreams do come true.

 Thought: What does Hogan want you never to give up?

Watch Hogan on YouTube
www.youtube.com/c/ConnieBombaci
https://tinyurl.com/FindingForeverHome
https://tinyurl.com/HogansFirstSigns

Connie Bombaci brings her multi-award-winning book, Hogan's Hope, to children of all ages. Hogan, a rescued deaf pup, teaches us all that being different makes us very special and that we are worthy of real love and genuine acceptance. With hope, anything is possible.

Connie has loved animals from early childhood and clearly remembers bringing home the orphaned, abandoned, or injured creatures who only wanted to be loved and cared for in their innocent lives. She holds fast to her belief that each precious creature blessed her life with greater joy and deeper understanding that each one of us needs to be embraced with gentle love and unwavering acceptance.

Her deepest gratitude goes to everyone who believes in the wonder of individual differences and unique characteristics. Hogan's determination taught her to live her life as a courageous journey, one step at a time, and she resolved that his life was going to be "A gift that keeps on giving." Hogan triumphed and revealed to the world that anything is possible when we remain steadfast in our hope.

Connect with Connie

www.conniebombaci.com

www.Facebook.com/ConnieBombaci

www.Twitter.com/ConnieBombaci

www.Instagram.com/ConnieBombaci

www.Youtube.com/c/ConnieBombaci

Watch Hogan on YouTube

Connie's Other Books

Secular Edition

Christian Edition

Children's Christian Edition

Heather Ferrer is the daughter of Connie Bombaci and shares her gift of art and creativity in this mother-daughter adventure for children. Heather's talents are widespread and include, but are not limited to, teaching, coaching, ministering, and understanding the hearts of others. Having been a world traveler, marine biologist, and veterinary technician for a wide variety of animals, she gained extensive experience and immeasurable compassion for the natural world that she freely shares to benefit those in need.

Heather cherishes and lives with her beautiful family in Connecticut.

 Answer from page 29: Hogan learned over 70 sign words!